RISEHOLME

KLIMKE ON
DRESSAGE

REINER KLIMKE · WERNER ERNST

KLIMKE ON
DRESSAGE
FROM THE YOUNG HORSE THROUGH GRAND PRIX

Half Halt Press, Inc.
Middletown, Maryland

Klimke on Dressage

Published in the United States of America by Half Halt Press, Inc.
6416 Burkittsville Road, Middletown, Maryland 21769

© 1992 HALF HALT PRESS, INC.
First published in Germany
© 1991 FRANCKH-KOSMOS VERLAG-GMBH, Stuggart
Original title: VON DER SCHÖNHEIT DER DRESSUR

Translated by Courtney Searls-Ridge and Jan Spauschus Johnson for
German Language Services, Seattle

Printed in Mexico

Table of Contents

Editors' Note

In many respects, the German equestrian vocabulary is much richer than our English. There are a number of descriptive terms in German for which there is simply no direct English equivalent. For that reason, we have used the German terms *takt* and *schwung* within this text.

Takt refers to the steady rhythm, or beats, of the horse's steps in all gaits, free of uneven strides, steps or little jumps.

Schwung is truly a special term, often simply translated as "impulsion," though it suggests so much more: the energy and elasticity of the steps, the desire to move forward, the suppleness of the horse's back, and the engagement of the hindquarters (see "Impulsion" in the Collective Marks on the FEI tests).

For another German term probably familiar to readers, *durchlassigheit*, we have used "throughness" or "through" as those words become more a part of the English dressage vernacular. The concept of "through" is more than simply an obedience or responsiveness to the aids, but conveys the concept of a straight horse allowing the action of the reins to come "through" the horse's whole body. The horse is listening and half-halts are effective. This allows for the maximum expression of the natural gaits.

One note on the comparison of the national competition levels, those below the FEI, may aid the reader. The German Class L is roughly equivalent to Second Level in the U.S., and the Elementary Level in the U.K. Class M is approximate to the U.S.'s Third Level, and the U.K.'s Medium Level. And Class S is equivalent to the U.S.'s Fourth and Fifth Levels and the U.K.'s Advanced Standard. Above these national levels, competitors world-wide share the same tests: Prix St. Georges, Intermédiaire I and II, and Grand Prix.

THE EDITORS

Foreword

Of the various forewords I've written, most were for books in whose realization I'd played some sort of real role. This one may be an exception, even though its author maintains that his latest work was actually my idea.

So let me set the record straight. I have been an admirer of Reiner Klimke for a very long time, not only because of his marvelous performances in the dressage arena, but also—in fact, especially—because of his generosity and patience as a trainer and teacher in sharing his profound knowledge of dressage with anyone who would bother to try to learn. I think I have learned a lot from Reiner myself, both from his books and the example of his riding, and since I have long been involved in equestrian publishing, it was only natural for me to try to come up with an idea that might tempt him to do another book.

In point of fact, this is not it. For what Reiner did was to take my kernel of idea and immediately transform it into something completely and characteristically his own—a book in picture and in word about the beauty of the sport to which he has devoted so much of his life. (Hence the title of the original German edition of the book: *Von der Schönheit der Dressur: Of the Beauty of Dressage.*) Even though I think Reiner would agree that the true beauty of dressage can only be seen in the movement of horse and rider, rather than in the necessarily static images on a printed page, every rider and student of dressage can learn a lot about what goes into a beautiful dressage performance from studying Werner Ernst's beautiful color photographs and Reiner Klimke's illuminating accompanying text. I am very grateful to Reiner for having shared his thoughts again with us in this handsome volume, and am sure that dressage enthusiasts everywhere will agree.

WILLIAM STEINKRAUS

Introduction

Dressage is not an invention of our times. It goes back thousands of years to the Classical equitation handed down to us from the time of Cimon and Xenophon (430-355 B.C.). In his books *The Art of Riding* and *The Cavalry* Major, Xenophon placed early emphasis on a supple and independent seat for riders. Xenophon was not concerned with basic training, since he viewed this as the responsibility of a rider specially trained for the task of breaking horses. Nevertheless, his instructions on the handling and schooling of the horse as a "state or parade horse" indicate his high degree of sensitivity, which even today would be a credit to many a rider.

Succeeding generations did not maintain the advanced equitation of the Greeks. It is said that even the Romans had a different attitude toward the horse. Sensitivity for the feelings of the horse faded into the background; the zeal of the masses demanded instant gratification.

The history of dressage over the following centuries was checkered, influenced by prevailing attitudes toward animals in general and by the use of horses in the service of humans. This history was also influenced by the build and type of horse of the time.

Today's dressage is based on the only remaining use of the horse, that of "sports equipment" for humans. The partnership between humankind and animal becomes the central focus. In training the horse we can draw on the discoveries of animal psychology and learn to take into consideration the personality of the horse.

Today, the feelings of people toward animals are in some ways so highly sensitized that one finds examples of an exaggerated love of animals, more important to some people than even the love of their own children. Regardless of how one feels about this problem, it is a certainty that the horse of our day has benefited from this development. The work horse used in war, for day work in mines, or for heavy pulling is a thing of the past. It is no longer necessary to train the horse to be a piece of machinery. Gymnastic training should make our dressage horses stronger, healthier, and more beautiful. The schooling in obedience to the rider's aids should be carried out with such sensitivity that the horse's happiness in his work is evident. This joy should carry over to the spectators; they should experience how an independently moving horse is presented by a rider using almost invisible aids.

This brings us to the purpose of this book. I want to show you the beauty and elegance of dressage with words and pictures. I invite you now to follow the development of the dressage horse from youngster to the maturity of the Grand Prix horse.

Critics may hold it against me that my models describe an ideal, and that in reality things often look very different. I don't deny this; it is, in fact, one of the reasons I have written this book. We need this image of the dressage horse, moving correctly and striving for perfection in harmony with the rider. Only then do we have a goal toward which to orient ourselves, one that at the same time exposes misuse.

We live in a time in which the breeders of riding horses have made great progress. Never before has the breeding industry given us horses whose conformation and temperament make them so well suited as perfect dressage horses. It is up to us to transform them into works of art.

Naturally, not every dressage rider or every dressage horse is predestined to reach the highest level of the Grand Prix. If in the course of training it becomes evident that there are limits to either the horse's or rider's predisposition, the performance level reached by that point should not be considered a loss. A dressage horse that's going well at Class L, one that's performing correctly at Class M, or one that is going well at Class S but displays no talent for piaffe and passage can still bring riders so much joy that the rider can and should be happy. It was therefore important to me to introduce not only the perfectly trained Grand Prix horse, but also the individual phases of the training leading up to it. Each of these represents a particular level of performance with which riders, depending on their ambitions, can be content. Not all dressage riders have to become world champions, but all of them can be happy if they limit themselves to goals that they and their horses can attain without jeopardizing their horse's health and well being.

The Goal of Dressage in Competition

The Federation Equestre Internationale (FEI) has laid down the rules of dressage competition in the special guidelines of its regulations (RG) for dressage. According to these, the goal of dressage is the harmonious development of the natural talents and abilities of the horse.

A properly adjusted snaffle is a prerequisite for a harmonious connection between the rider's hand and the horse's mouth.
The Trakehner stallion Pinot by Waldzauber, the very picture of eagerness to perform.

When using a double bridle, the correct positioning of the snaffle and the curb is crucial to satisfactory acceptance of the bit.
The French crossbreed stallion Bibelo by Bibelot standing proudly at attention.

This sentence alone is only a part of the description, because it applies also to the training of jumpers and event horses. Therefore the following description includes a list of the qualities of the well-trained dressage horse, which I will examine more closely.

The Difference Between Dressage and Circus Riding

By rejecting the teaching of artificial movements, the RG of the FEI distinguishes between dressage riding in competition and other forms of dressage. Circus dressage includes these types of movements. For example, in the circus we see dressage horses that dance the rumba or the polka, passage, and perform a variety of tricks, from kneeling to counting to climbing. This is not to say anything derogatory about dressage riding in the circus; today's competitive dressage had its beginning there. Around the turn of the century, before there were dressage tests at horse shows, renowned dressage riders demonstrated their skills in the circus with the applauding audience as their judge.

Borrowed from Nature

The rules of the FEI dictate that in dressage competition only the horse's natural movements—primarily the three basic gaits: walk, trot, and canter—should be given greater expression and lightness. In addition, only movements and exercises that one sees horses perform on their own in the open—albeit only briefly—have been included in dressage tests. For example, when changing directions at the canter, horses normally switch leads; this is how the flying change originated. Or we see how the horse that's just been turned out shows off a prancing trot; this becomes the passage.

One can continue with examples like these for almost every movement in the dressage tests. The philosophy behind this is clear: we want to develop the horse's natural movements from the three basic gaits—walk, trot, and canter—and leave it at that.

Airs Above the Ground

Airs above the ground, like those performed by the Lippizans at the Spanish Riding School in Vienna, are not included in international dressage competition. The reason for this, as expressly stated in the FEI's RG, is that in many countries these movements are no longer cultivated.

The qualities of a correctly trained dressage horse are expressed by:
- freedom and regularity of the gaits;
- harmony, lightness, and ease of movement;
- submission and responsiveness to the most discrete rider aids;
- naturalness of the whole performance, as though no effort were required of horse or rider.

The training of the dressage horse, from young horse to Grand Prix, takes approximately 4 to 6 years. During this time gymnastic training should allow the horse to mature into a healthy athlete whose carriage is proud and confident, and who moves with suppleness and looseness, proper *takt*, *schwung*, and straightness.

As this goal is reached, the horse's appearance will continue to change. The keen observer can judge a horse's training level by the overall picture he presents. A 4-year-old horse moves differently compared to a 6-year-old after two years of training. The level of maturity increases throughout training, and this is visible in the overall impression.

The personality of the horse must remain recognizable through all phases of training. Should the horse's enthusiasm about his work—his radiance—wane, it should be a warning sign for the rider. The rider must tailor the challenges to the horse's fitness level.

The 4-Year-Old Horse at Class A

Horses are started in training in about their third year. The exact time for this is determined by their physical growth; in particular, the joints, bones, and tendons should be almost fully developed.

In the first phase of training, the horse has to learn to adjust to the unfamiliar weight of the rider on his back. He must acquire the ability to move as freely and naturally with the rider in the saddle as he did before, without the rider. This places demand on the horse's back muscles, which have to be suppled on the one hand and strengthened on the other, so that the horse can carry and balance the rider's weight, allowing him to retain his natural action. In the jargon of the trade we describe this with the terms suppleness and looseness and *takt*.

By suppleness and looseness we mean a horse freely gives all his muscles and uses his whole body. By *takt* we mean the steady rhythm of the movements, free of uneven strides, steps, or jumps.

Next we turn our attention to gaining influence over the horse's movements. Whereas during early training the rider concentrates on not letting her weight interfere and in adjusting smoothly to the rhythm of the horse's movements, she now becomes an active partner by attempting with the use of aids to transform the horse into an athlete.

We differentiate between weight, leg, and rein aids. Each of these aids is generally most effective when used in harmony with the others, rather than singly. A good rider, therefore, doesn't simply ride with the reins, but instead combines these aids with leg pressure and a shift in weight, for example, in order to have an optimal effect on the horse.

Obviously it takes some time for the horse to become accustomed to the rider's weight, leg, and rein aids. We have to explain these aids to the young horse, get him to accept them and respond to them. We refer to this phase of training as basic schooling, which takes approximately a year and concludes with the goal of reaching Class A.

Certain lessons and exercises are used in every phase of training to help teach the horse to submit to the rider's aids. These are not ends in themselves but rather means to an end, namely aids to train the appropriate muscles of the horse, partly to supple them and partly to strengthen them. I want to emphasize here that dressage schooling must go beyond producing schooling "machines." Riders who only practice schooling exercises dull their horses and wear down their gaits. The way in which the rider succeeds in bringing out the grace and beauty of the horse in each required exercise is what gives a performance its brilliance. Then we are on the threshold of the art of riding.

In the preliminary schooling of the young horse, after the initial breaking and the period of adjustment to the rider's aids, we need a link between the rider's hand and the horse's mouth in order to gain control of the horse's movements. In dressage terms we call this riding with contact. The horse should learn to step up into the reins. By doing so he gains the self carriage—appropriate to his length of stride—in which he can best develop his abilities.

One can discern the horse's level of training from his frame and self carriage. In a 4-year-old horse, the neck muscles and the weight-bearing capacity of the hindquarters have just begun to develop. The hind legs are not quite "closed," or engaged, and the neck is raised only a little. At this stage of training, the rider must use great sensitivity so as not to demand too much too soon. Unfortunately, in competition—even in Class A tests—we often see horses with overbent necks. The results are rigid back muscles and a blocking of the rear legs. Instead of gaining greater expression, the horse's movements are restrained. The horses' gaits are worn down, rather than improved.

The natural expression of a young dressage horse at the walk on a loose rein.
Kim Keenan (USA) on the Dutch gelding Deja Vu by Ulster.

The young dressage horse at a medium walk on the bit. The contact is soft and steady, the rider's hands are held low. The horse is moving correctly through the poll. The nose remains in front of the vertical.
Brett Moon (USA) on the Hessian gelding Eglant by Egmont.

The 5-Year-Old Horse at Class L

The young dressage horse develops from Class A into the training phase of Class L in about the fifth year. Here our goals are:

- The contact between the rider's hand and the horse's mouth should be strengthened further. We want a soft and steady connection on both reins.
- The horse's submission to the weight, leg, and rein aids increases; this applies primarily to the forward-driving and regulating aids. Dressage riders call this "throughness," or being "through."
- Throughness leads to strengthening the muscles in the hindquarters allowing them to carry more weight. This in turn takes weight off the forehand and allows greater freedom in the shoulder.

The movements in Class L tests include basic exercises that lead to the goals described above.

The Half Halt

A key lesson in the schooling toward all Class L goals, one that has its beginnings in Class A, is that of half halts, used in the transitions within a gait or from one gait to another. Here the half halt fulfills the function of briefly transferring the center of gravity to the haunches and bringing about a yielding in the poll.

Through frequent transitions from the trot to the walk or—primarily at Class L—from the canter to the walk, the horse practices shifting his center of gravity. By doing so, he gains lightness of step and suppleness.

The Full Halt

Full halts are the continuation of half halts and lead to a complete stop. While for the halt at Class A it is sufficient to have the horse stand immobile on all four legs, at Class L this should be marked by a higher degree of engagement. The horse should not only stand immobile on all four legs and on a straight line, he must also distribute the weight equally over all four legs, and stand square. If, for example, when positioned for the salute one of the rear legs lags behind, this shows that the horse has not distributed his weight equally over all four legs.

The Rein-back

An important measure of the horse's throughness at Class L is the rein-back. The rein-back is demanded of the 4-year-old horse as a test of obedience. In Class L dressage, however, more is required: the horse should step backward in a two-beat rhythm, alternating diagonal pairs of legs, with each hoof leaving the ground distinctly, and should do so in a straight line, willingly, and with steps of equal length.

The Turn on the Haunches and Half-Pirouette in Walk

The turn on the haunches addresses the throughness and the initial collection of the horse at Class L. Collection means that the hind legs carry more weight as a result of increased flexion in the haunches.

The half-pirouette is begun from the halt. The forehand traces a half-circle around the haunches as the horse moves in collected walk around the inside hind leg, which is raised and lowered with every step and not allowed to stand still. In the pirouette, the sequence of steps is the same as in the half-pirouette, except that the horse does not come to a halt before, during, or after the turn. The horse's head is turned and the neck bent slightly in the direction in which the horse is making the turn.

Top right: The 4-year-old horse in natural self carriage at the working trot. The horse is just beginning to become engaged with natural, balanced movements. The rider uses a rising trot, hands set low, resulting in a the horse with a lovely neck carriage.
Ingrid Klimke on the Trakehner Kronjuwel by Mahagoni in 1988 at the Turnier der Sieger in Münster.

Bottom right: The working trot of the 5-year-old horse. The horse moves according to his natural abilities, without a trace of tension and with exemplary neck carriage.
Dr. Reiner Klimke on the Westphalian Patriot by Palast in 1989 at the Mannheim Maimarktturnier.

The Counter-Canter and Simple Change of Lead

The degree of difficulty of canter work in Class L dressage is characterized by the counter-canter and the simple change of lead. The counter-canter demands better balance and equilibrium. The horse should learn to maintain the rhythm of the canter movement in the same way as at a true canter.

In the simple change of lead the horse's hind legs absorb all the weight he is carrying as he goes without any trot strides from a canter into a walk. Following three to five well-defined walk strides, the transition is made back to the canter, again without trotting.

Expression of Movement

We know that the Class L lessons described above are only tools to help increase the elegance of the horse and the expression of his movements. This must be visible from the overall presentation of the horse during the dressage test. The medium trot and medium canter of the Class L horse must distinguish themselves clearly from those of a Class A horse by a greater degree of development. Only then is the rider's training on the right track.

We estimate that it takes at least one year to reach the Class L stage of training. It can easily take another year for the horse to garner enough proficiency in Class L tests for him to display what he has learned confidently under competitive conditions.

Top right: The young dressage horse at a working canter on the right lead. Expressive canter stride of a contented horse ridden in a closed frame.
Kim Keenan (USA) on the Dutch gelding Deja Vu by Ulster.

Bottom right: Michael Klimke on the Dutch gelding Frederik by Ulft. The inside hind leg is well underneath the horse. Good upward movement of the canter stride.

The young dressage horse at a working canter.
Various phases of the canter on the left lead:

Above: Following the moment of suspension, the right
hind foot is the first to touch down.

Top right: The left hind foot and right front foot prepare
to set down.

Bottom right: The left hind foot and right front foot
touch down simultaneously with the left front foot
distinctly angled. The rider supports the horse's
movements with a sensitive influence.
Ralf Isselhorst on the Westphalian gelding Webster
by Walldorf.

Riding into corners correctly at the trot.
Tracking right: Brett Moon (USA) on the Hessian
gelding Eglant by Egmont. Corners are ridden by
following the shape of a quarter volte. The horse is
bent around the inside leg.

Canter circle to the right.
Good bend in the horse's body. The right hind foot is placed well underneath. The forehand is a bit over elevated. The inside rein could be lighter.
Brett Moon (USA) on the Hessian gelding Eglant by Egmont.

Canter circle to the left.
On the circle at the center of the arena, a working canter with energetic upward movement.
Uta Erpenstein on the Wesphalian gelding Fitou by Frederiko.

The halt and salute.
The rider takes both reins in the left hand in preparation for the salute. The horse's position remains unchanged as he stands quietly on all four feet. The right hind foot is a bit out of line.

The same halt for the salute, this time perfectly straight.
Uta Erpenstein on the Westphalian gelding Fitou by Frederiko.

The 6-Year-Old Horse at Class M

In his sixth year the dressage horse graduates to Class M. At this level of training we improve the equal development of the horse on both sides through lateral movements. In the canter work, the horse learns the flying change. Collection and *schwung* are increased, lending greater expression to the horse's action. The horse presents himself more naturally.

The rider's aids become less obvious once the horse understands the new exercises. As in Class L, one can therefore also distinguish between the training to reach a particular level and the subsequent reinforcement of what has been learned until the required movements can be carried out independently.

Lateral Movements

Lateral movements comprise shoulder-in, haunches-in, haunches-out, and half-pass. In these, the horse moves with the forehand and hindquarters on two tracks, forward and sideways. He is bent laterally. Bend, *takt*, tempo, and *schwung* are maintained.

The Shoulder-in

In the shoulder-in, the horse's hind legs remain on the outside track. The forehand is brought just enough to the inside that the horse's outside shoulder is in front of his inside hip. From the front we then see three tracks. The horse is flexed and bent laterally away from the direction in which he is moving.

The value of the shoulder-in exercise in schooling also lies in the fact that the rider can use the diagonal aids to improve the horse's straightness. Diagonal aids mean here that the rider drives the horse with the inside leg against the outside controlling rein, thereby straightening the horse relative to himself.

The Haunches-in (Travers)

In the haunches-in, the horse is flexed and bent in the direction in which he is moving. The forehand remains on the outside track. The haunches are shifted to the inside, so that from the front one sees four tracks.

The Haunches-out (Renvers)

The haunches-out is a reversed haunches-in. Here the forehand is brought to the inside. The hindquarters stay on the outside track. Otherwise the same rules apply as in the haunches-in.

The Half-Pass

The half-pass is a variation of the haunches-in but is executed on a diagonal line, approximately parallel to the long side of the arena. The horse must be perfectly balanced in order to maintain an even bend and to move sideways with proper *takt* and *schwung*; therefore this movement can only be demanded once the horse has fully mastered the challenges of Class L.

Class M requires half-passes across half the width of the arena and down half its length, and double half-passes (a half-pass in one direction down half the length of the arena, followed immediately by a half-pass in the other direction down the remaining half). Later the requirements are increased to include half-passes across the full width of the arena and zigzags down the center line.

A trainer can consider it a compliment to receive confirmation that a horse being shown at Class M fulfills all the requirements mentioned for the half-pass in both directions. Good half-passes in both directions also influence the quality of the extensions at the trot as well as the canter. In Class M dressage they are the most reliable measure of a horse's level of training.

The Flying Change

The dressage horse that learned at Class L to balance himself in the counter-canter in both directions is ready for flying changes. In the flying change, the horse changes leads during the moment of suspension in the canter. The forehand and hindquarters switch simultaneously on a straight line.

The dressage horse that has advanced to Class M, at the medium walk on the bit. The horse's muscles already show definite contour, especially along the top of the neck. Michael Klimke on the Dutch gelding The Carlos by Statuar.

The tempo and the horse's carriage remain unchanged.

If the croup is thrown upward during the change, it is a sign that the horse is still uneasy about the rider's new aids. It often takes weeks or months before a horse can carry out a flying change with the requisite composure. Experience teaches us that practicing the flying change initially makes horses somewhat agitated, especially because they just learned not to switch leads when practicing the counter-canter at the previous level. It is therefore no cause for alarm if the horse that is learning the flying change loses some of the quality of the canter stride to tension.

I recommend that when practicing the flying change in the training phase of Class M dressage it not be repeated too often in the same spot. Instead, a simple change of lead should be ridden every now and then in order to renew the horse's confidence in the aids. Trust and sensitivity are particularly important now for reestablishing harmony between horse and rider following this temporary agitation. This is the only way to master Class M, which demands a great deal of riding skill.

Working with Nature

Before ending this chapter on Class M training, I would like to emphasize its developmental value. This is the turning point for some horses. From this point on much will depend on the horse's degree of intelligence and whether or not it is sufficient for completion of the next level.

As I noted earlier, nature may have set limits to the horse's ability to move well. These days almost every correctly built horse can be developed enough to perform a clean Class M test. Only now, though, does it become evident whether or not the horse will develop the ability to learn and the capacity of stride needed to reach Class S. This aptitude is very difficult to predict in 3- or 4-year-old horses; thus the selection process that takes place over the course of training is—unfortunately—one of elimination. Optimism increases from one training level to the next. By Class M at the very latest, it becomes clear to what extent the gaits can be developed through proper training.

The stopping point may now have been reached. This or that can still be improved, but the critical momentum is missing. Here nature has set a limit. The dressage trainer confronted with such a situation has to recognize this and act accordingly. She cannot succumb to the temptation to undertake a futile attempt to use force, if necessary, to get more out of a horse than nature gave him to begin with.

A satisfied Class M horse is always worth more than one improperly forced to Class S. We should remind ourselves how many riders we can make happy with a properly trained and contented Class M horse; then no further comment is needed.

The training goal for the Class M dressage horse can be summarized as follows:

- The horse is absolutely straight; here we are helped primarily by the diagonal aids in the shoulder-in exercise;

- The mobility of the horse at the canter is improved by learning the flying change;

- The muscles in the haunches become stronger, increasing their weight-bearing capacity. The degree of collection becomes more developed, and with it the horse's lightness and suppleness in his sequence of movements;

- It becomes evident whether there is enough *schwung* and expression available to meet increased demands.

Top right: A working trot with increasing engagement.
The right hind foot is lifted energetically, transferring schwung *along the back to the shoulder, allowing it to swing freely. This is the way the working trot of the Class M horse—with the requisite ability—should look.*
Michael Klimke on the Dutch gelding The Carlos by Statuar.

Bottom right: The medium trot with exemplary takt *and* schwung.
The horse's neck could be a little less restrained.
Michael Klimke on the Dutch gelding The Carlos by Statuar.

A correct halt for the dressage horse in training at Class M.
On the center line in the middle of the arena, the horse is standing square, with weight distributed evenly over all 4 legs. The eyes and ears are forward. The contact remains unchanged. A good example of the proper rider's seat.
Michael Klimke on the Dutch gelding The Carlos by Statuar.

The halt on the center line, perfectly straight, with horse and rider in harmony.
Michael Klimke on the Dutch gelding The Carlos by Statuar.

The shoulder-in left as performed by the young dressage horse in Class M training. The rider brings the horse's forehand far enough to the inside that the outside shoulder is in front of the inside hip. The horse is flexed and bent slightly to the left.
Inza Hansen on the Oldenburg mare Raphael's Lady by Raphael.

A nearly perfect shoulder-in right.
Nicole Uphoff on the Hanoverian gelding Sir Lenox by Shogun xx, a picture that communicates the correct development of the properly trained dressage horse: light, expressive, forehand nicely elevated, well flexed and bent.

The shoulder-in and half-pass improve the horse's suppleness on both sides.

Half-pass to the left. The horse moves parallel to the long side of the arena and looks in the direction in which he is moving. A good crossing over of the legs at the trot tempo. The flexion and bend could be more pronounced.

Michael Klimke on the Hanoverian stallion Alpius by Akzent.

Half-pass to the right. A successful execution in which everything is correct: energetic crossing over of alternate pairs of legs, good flexion and bend, and good influence by the rider, whose seat moves with the horse.

Michael Klimke on the Hanoverian stallion Alpius by Akzent.

A study of a talented young dressage horse at the trot.

Top left: A working trot with full expression.

Bottom left: A medium trot with natural schwung and lovely self-carriage.

Above: The extended trot: the energetic lifting of the feet produces a marked increase of schwung in an attentive horse, with the forehand lightened and elevated.
Ralf Isselhorst on the Westphalian gelding Webster by Waldorf.

The Dressage Horse at Class S

The well-trained dressage horse reaches the performance rank of Class S with the challenges of the Prix St. Georges approximately between his sixth and seventh years. At this stage we have several national and international levels of training, ranging from Prix St. Georges to the Intermédiaire I and II programs, to the most difficult, the Grand Prix, Grand Prix Special, and Freestyle Grand Prix. The first two tests, Prix St. Georges and Intermédiaire I, can be described as introductory steps to this level, while Intermédiaire II shows once and for all whether a dressage horse will learn the movements requiring the utmost degree of collection, namely piaffe and passage.

Prix St. Georges

As described in the FEI dressage regulations, this test should demonstrate the dressage horse's suitability to the demands of Classical equitation. The movements are more difficult than those of Class M. In addition to lateral movements at the trot, half-passes at the canter are required. Flying changes are now required at various tempi, namely 5 changes every 4 strides and 5 changes every 3 strides. From the program of collected movements, the Prix St. Georges test includes the half-pirouette at a canter. Overall it is clear that a greater degree of gymnastic ability should be reflected in the expression of the horse's movements.

The Flying Change Every 4 and 3 Strides

When performing flying changes at various tempi, the horse should stay on a straight line and remain calm and light in the hand while maintaining a lively forward drive. The rhythm of the canter strides should remain unchanged. The degree of collection is adjusted to the tempo in order to avoid a shortening of the canter strides and to allow each change to spring forth lightly.

The Half-Pirouette at a Canter

In the half-pirouette at the canter, the horse should canter, in three to four strides, in as small a half-circle as possible around the haunches while sustaining the *takt* and tempo of the gait. The horse should be flexed and bent in the direction in which he is moving. The haunches are lowered through the increased degree of collection. The importance of this movement in the training program is emphasized by the fact that the half-pirouette at the canter is assigned a coefficient of 2 in the scoring scale, thereby doubling its value.

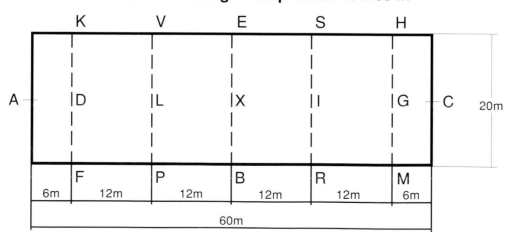

Arena for Dressage Competition 20 x 60 m

Prix St. Georges

Arena 20 x 60m—Approximately 7 minutes.

			Coefficient
1.	A	Enter in collected canter	
	X	Halt, immobility, salute. Proceed in collected trot	
2.	C	Track to the right	
	MXK	Chang rein at extended trot	
	K	Collected trot	
3.	FB	Shoulder-in to the left	
4.	B	Circle to the left 8m diameter	
5.	BG	Half-pass	
	G	On center line	
	C	Track to the right	
6.	MF	Medium trot	
	F	Collected trot	
7.	KE	Shoulder-in to the right	
8.	E	Circle to the right 8m diameter	
9.	EG	Half-pass	
	G	On center line	
	C	Track to the left	
10.	HXF	Change rein in extended trot	
	F	Collected trot	
11.	AKR	Change rein in extended walk	2
12.	R	Collected walk	
	M	Turn left	
	Between		
	G & H	Half-pirouette to the left	
13.	Between		
	G & M	Half-pirouette to the right	
14.		The collected walk RMG (H) (M) GHC	
15.	C	Proceed in collected canter right	
16.	RI	Half-circle of 10m diameter left followed by half-circle	
	IS	left in counter-canter	
	SE	Counter-canter	
	E	Flying change of leg	
17.	VL	Half-circle of 10m diameter left followed by half-circle	
	LP	right in counter-canter	
	PF	Counter-canter	
	F	Flying change of leg	
18.	KXM	On the diagonal 5 flying changes of leg every 4th stride	
19.	H	Proceed toward X in collected canter	
	Between		
	H & X	Half-pirouette to the left	2
	H	Flying change of leg	
20.	M	Proceed toward X in collected canter	
	Between		
	M & X	Half-pirouette to the right	2
	M	Flying change of leg	

			Coefficient
21.	HXF	Change rein in medium canter	
	F	Collected canter and flying change of leg	
22.	KX	Half-pass	
	XI	On center line	
23.	I	Halt, rein back 4 steps and immediately proceed in collected canter left	
	C	Track to the left	
24.	HX	Half-pass	
	X	On center line	
	L	Flying change of leg	
	A	Track to the right	
25.	KXM	Change rein in extended canter	
	M	Collected canter and flying change of leg	
26.	HXF	On the diagonal 5 flying changes of leg every 3rd stride	
27.	A	Down center line	
	X	Halt, immobility, salute	

Collective Marks

		Coefficient
28.	Paces (freedom and regularity)	2
29.	Impulsion (desire to move forward, elasticity of the steps, suppleness of the back and engagement of the hindquarters)	2
30.	Submission (attention and confidence; harmony, lightness and ease of the movements; acceptance of the bridle and lightness of the forehand)	2
31.	Rider's position and seat; correctness and effect of the aids	2

Possible Points: 380

The collected canter to the right, with utmost concentration.
Christine Stückelberger (Switzerland) on the Holsteiner gelding Granat by Consul at the1976 Olympic Games in Bromont (Canada). They were winners of the individual gold medal.

A flying change from the right lead to the left, with excellent expression of the left front leg.
Gina Capellmann-Lütkemeyer on the Dutch gelding Ampere by Amagun, member of the 1986 world champion team in Cedar Valley (Canada).

The flying change from the right to the left lead, with the left hind leg reaching well under the horse.
Margit Otto-Crepin (France) on the Holsteiner gelding Corlandus by Cor de la Bryere.

A half-pass to the left, fully balanced, in three-beat canter rhythm.
Dr. Uwe Schulten-Baumer on the Hanoverian gelding Slibovitz by Servus, runner-up at the 1978 world championships in Goodwood (England).

A full pirouette to the right, on as tight a circle and with as much collection as possible.
Elisabeth Theurer-Max (Austria) on the Oldenburg gelding Mon Cherie by Inshalla, Olympic champion in 1980 in Moscow.

Two stallions demonstrating ultimate schwung at the trot.
Top right: Karin Rehbein on the Oldenburg stallion Donnerhall by Donnerwetter in 1989 in Rotterdam. The execution of this extended trot is the result of proper dressage training. The horse has matured into an athlete. Well-muscled in the hindquarters, back, neck, and shoulder, he displays his full capacity of stride.

Bottom right: Pia Laus on the Westphalian stallion Adrett by Adlerfest is every bit Donnerhall's match. The energetic lifting of the left hind leg as a factor in the increase of schwung is expressed even more clearly.

Herbert Krug on the Swedish gelding Muscadeur, member of the gold-medal team at the 1984 Olympics in Los Angeles. A fully extended trot just before entering the arena for the Grand Prix. Excellent harmony between horse and rider.

Intermédiaire I

FEI dressage regulations describe the Intermédiaire I test as being for those horses that have correctly mastered the Prix St. Georges and are to be prepared for the more difficult Intermédiaire II test gradually and without endangering their health. Horses reach this stage in their seventh or eighth year. The following movements are added to those of the Prix St. Georges: the rein-back sequence, canter zigzags down the center line, flying changes every two strides, and full pirouettes. The trot and walk work is the same as in the Prix St. Georges.

The Rein-back Sequence

In the rein-back sequence, the horse takes four steps backward from a halt, then without stopping takes four steps forward, another four steps backward—again, without stopping—and then strikes off in a collected canter.

This movement requires a great deal of throughness and collection from the horse. The backward steps must be taken with alternating diagonal pairs of legs (in two-beat rhythm). The forward steps are done at a normal walk (in four-beat rhythm). The transitions should be fluid and effortless. The horse should perform the exercise calmly, maintaining his proud carriage and supported by the rider only with soft, barely discernible aids.

The Canter Zigzag

The zigzag down the center line can only be done correctly at the canter by a perfectly balanced horse that has been schooled equally in both directions. The Intermédiaire I test requires zigzags at the canter: At the canter on the left lead, four strides to the left, followed by a flying change; then eight strides to the right, followed by a flying change and eight strides to the left; then a flying change to the right and four strides to the right. Finally, straight ahead and flying change to the left.

The rhythm of the canter must be maintained throughout the entire movement. The horse is bent in the direction of the canter. The flying change in between is performed with perfect straightness.

The rapid succession and exact limit of the prescribed strides, along with the intervening changes and the adjustment of the horse to the new direction, also place great demands on the rider. If the rider fails to keep exact count and hesitates with the aids for even a fraction of a second, the horse will lose the rhythm and the success of the whole movement will be jeopardized. Step by step, the challenges facing the rider increase also.

The Canter Pirouette

In the canter pirouette, the horse must canter around the haunches, in as small a circle as possible, in about 6 to 8 strides. The hindquarters are lowered due to the greater degree of collection and carry more of the weight. The rhythm of the canter remains virtually unchanged. The horse is flexed and bent slightly to the inside.

The Flying Change Every 2 Strides

In the Intermédiaire I program, the demands of the flying changes at various tempi are increased from those of the Prix St. Georges to 7 changes every 2 strides. Normally this increase causes little difficulty, because a horse that in the Prix St. Georges learned to execute the changes correctly every 3 strides will quickly learn the more rapid succession up to 2 strides if the rider maintains quiet and does not force the horse.

Intermédiaire I

Arena 20 x 60m—Approximately 6 minutes.

The following movements are demanded for the first time in Intermédiaire I:

The rein-back sequence

Canter zigzags down the center line

Full pirouettes

Flying changes every two strides

			Coefficient
I.	A	Enter in collected canter	
	X	Halt, immobility, salute. Proceed in collected trot	
2.	C	Track to the left	
	HE	Shoulder-in to the left	
3.	EF	Change rein in medium trot	
	FAK	Collected trot	
4.	KE	Shoulder-in to the right	
5.	EM	Change rein in medium trot	
	MCH	Collected trot	
6.	HXF	Change rein in extended trot	
	F	Collected trot	
7.	A	Down center line	
	DB	Half-pass to the right	
8.	BG	Half-pass to the left	
	G	On center line	
9.	Before		
	C	Collected walk	
	C	Track to the left	
	H	Track to the left	
	Between		
	G & M	Half-pirouette to the left	
10.	Between		
	G & H	Half-pirouette to the right	
11.		The collected walk CHGM	
12.	MRXV	Change rein in extended walk	
	V	Collected walk	2
13.	VKD	Collected walk	

46

			Coefficient
14.	D	Halt, rein back 4 steps, forward 4 steps, rein back 4 steps and immediately proceed in collected canter right	
	F	Track to the right	
15		Transitions from collected walk to halt and from rein back to collected canter	
16.	KXM	Change rein in medium canter with flying change of leg at X	
	M	Collected canter	
17.	CA	Serpentine 5 loops, first and second true canter, third in counter canter, fourth and fifth in true canter with flying changes of leg when crossing center line, ending at A on left rein	
18.	A	Down center line	'
	DG	3 counter changes half-pass to either side of the center line with change of leg at each change of direction; the 1st half-pass to the left and the last to the right of 4 strides; the two others of 8 strides	
	G	Flying change of leg	
	C	Track to the left	
19.	HXF	Change rein in extended canter	2
	F	Collected canter and flying change of leg	
20.	KB	On the diagonal	
	L	Pirouette right	
21.	B	Flying change of leg	
22.	BH	On the diagonal	2
	I	Pirouette left	
23.	H	Flying change of leg	
	HCM	Collected canter	
24.	MXK	On the diagonal 5 flying changes every 3rd stride	

			Coefficient
	KAF	Collected canter	
25.	FXH	On the diagonal 7 flying changes every 2nd stride	
	HCM	Collected canter	
26.	MXK	Change rein in extended canter	
	K	Collected canter and flying change of leg	
27.	A	Down center line	
	X	Halt, immobility, salute	

Collective Marks

		Coefficient
28.	Paces (freedom and regularity)	2
29.	Impulsion (desire to move forward, elasticity of the steps, suppleness of the back and engagement of the hindquarters)	2
30.	Submission (attention and confidence; harmony, lightness and ease of the movements; acceptance of the bridle and lightness of the forehand)	2
31.	Rider's position and seat; correctness and effect of the aids	2

Possible Points: 380

Arena for Dressage Competition 20 x 60m

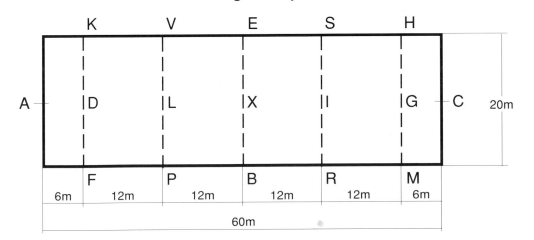

The transition to half-pass right.
Margit Otto-Crepin (France) on the Holsteiner gelding Corlandus by Cor de la Bryere in a picture-perfect transition into half-pass to the right. The rider flexes the horse slightly to the right and uses the inside leg to keep the schwung in the movement. The horse responds to the aids and, ears up, looks in the new direction.

The half-pass across the full width of the arena. Klaus Balkenhol on the Westphalian gelding Goldstern by Weinberg, a perfect example of bend, takt, and increase of schwung *throughout the entire half-pass to the left.*

A half-pass to the right across the entire arena. Christine Stückelberger (Switzerland) on the Swedish stallion Gauguin de Lully by Chagall; perfect flexion, bend, takt, and schwung.

The half-pass to the left across the entire arena, from movement 5 of the Grand Prix Special. A model of correct execution: Monica Theodorescu on the Westphalian gelding Ganimedes by Grünhorn.

A side view of the half-pass to the left across the full arena.
Performed correctly, with lovely harmony between horse and rider: Gina Capellmann-Lütkemeyer on the Dutch gelding Ampere by Amagun during the 1986 world championships in Cedar Valley (Canada).

A collected trot with expression.
Michael Klimke on the Rhinelander gelding Pitt
Ramos by Roman in the Prix St. Georges in 1989
in Rotterdam.

An exemplary example of schwung at the
extended trot.
Heike Kemmer on the Hanoverian gelding
Borsalino by Bolero at Intermédiaire I level.
Borsalino is one of few horses ever to score a
perfect 10 in the extended trot.

Canter pirouettes demand the highest degree of collection at the canter. The horse should canter around the hindquarters in approximately 6 to 8 strides, making the smallest circle possible. The hindquarters are lowered and take on increased weight. The horse is lightly flexed and bent to the inside.

Dr. Reiner Klimke on the Westphalian gelding Rocco Granata by Rokkoko in a full pirouette to the left. The canter stride on a small circle is well defined. The weight is on the hindquarters. Flexion and bend are visible. The rider supports the horse with the seat by going with the motion of the turn.

Isabell Werth on the Westphalian mare Fabienne by Feuerschein, also in the pirouette to the left. This photo shows the pirouette at the next phase of the movement: the inside hind is just being set down again and distribution of weight, as well as the flexion and bend, are flawless. The collection in the neck is somewhat exaggerated, however.

The ability to ride the corners of the dressage arena correctly is an indication of the level of training.
Dr. Reiner Klimke on the Westphalian gelding Ahlerich by Angelo xx in Olympic dressage competition. The horse is flexed and bent to the inside. The corner is ridden along the curve of a quarter volte.

Intermédiaire II

When the dressage horse has mastered the Intermédiaire I program, he has reached the second to last step in his training. Now is the time to decide whether the horse's gaits and talent qualify him for training for the highest level, the challenge of the Grand Prix. The FEI created the Intermédiaire II program as training for this. The horses are now approximately eight years old. They become familiarized with the demands of the piaffe and passage and must learn to do the flying change at every stride.

Not every dressage horse has the aptitude for piaffe and passage. We observe this even in horses that have won against stiff competition in the Prix St. Georges and Intermédiaire I tests. The dressage horse's ability to collect for piaffe and passage is not just a matter of conformation and build, nor is it simply a question of proper training. There are horses whose inner qualities limit their ability to learn the piaffe and passage. This depends, among other things, on their eagerness to go forward and their temperament. If nature has set limits here, even the most patient trainer will not be able to coax perfect piaffes and passages from the horse. Applying force with such horses is even more useless. Force and harmony are enemies. Force can never generate harmony between horse and rider.

Conforming to the Classical School

The Intermédiaire II dressage program takes into account the gradual introduction of the dressage horse to the lessons of the piaffe and passage. The piaffe and passage are not required out in the open—as they are later, in the Grand Prix—but are instead performed on the outside track. This makes the work easier and puts us on the right path. The passage is required from a trot, making it easier to develop *schwung*. The piaffe is performed from a walk. This conforms to the classical school, according to which the piaffe should be developed by taking half-steps forward in a collected walk. Therefore the Intermédiaire II test specifically allows 1 meter of forward movement for the 7 to 8 steps of the piaffe.

The Piaffe

The piaffe is a trot-like movement performed in place. It belongs to the movements of the classical high school. The horse lifts alternate diagonal pairs of legs with well-defined cadence. The forearms are lifted approximately to the horizontal. The hind legs step energetically and are lifted to about the level of the fetlocks. The horse's carriage is proud, with the poll as the highest point. The urge to move forward should be evident in every step.

The Passage

The passage represents the highest level of collection and cadence at the trot. Stepping in the same order as at the trot, the alternating pairs of legs spring up energetically from the ground, prolonging the moment of suspension. As in the piaffe, the forearm should be raised to the horizontal. The horse's hind legs absorb and propel the weight straight forward and upward, doing so steadily and with proper *takt* while following exactly the track of the front legs. These may well be the proudest and most beautiful moments in the presentation of a well-trained horse demonstrating the highest degree of collection.

The Flying Change at Every Stride

The flying change at every stride is the most demanding of the changes in the Grand Prix. Nine of them are required in the Intermédiaire II test, and fifteen of them later on in the Grand Prix. The increase in the level of performance from the change every 2 strides to the change at every stride is greater than the one from 3-time to 2-time changes between Prix St. Georges and Intermédiaire I. There are horses that require a very long time before they are balanced enough at the canter to trust themselves to do the change at every stride. The intelligence of the horse must play a part in this movement; otherwise insurmountable problems can arise.

Intermédiaire II

Arena 20 x 60m—Approximately 6 minutes

			Coefficient
1.	A X C	Enter in collected canter Halt, immobility, salute. Proceed in collected trot Track to the right	
2.	MXK K	Change rein in extended trot Collected trot	
3.	FLE	Half-pass to the left	
4.	EIM MCH	Half-pass to the right Collected trot	
5.	HP P	Change rein in medium trot Collected trot	
6.	Between P & F FA	Proceed in passage Passage	
7.	A	Piaffe 7 to 8 steps (1 m forward permitted) and immediately proceed in collected trot	
8.		Transitions from passage to piaffe and from piaffe to collected trot	
9.	AK KR R	Collected trot Change rein in extended trot Collected walk	
10.	RMC	Collected walk	
11.	C	Piaffe 7 to 8 steps (1 m forward permitted) and immediately proceed in passage	
12.	CH	Passage	

The following movements are required for the first time in Intermédiaire II:

Flying changes at every stride

Piaffe

Passage

No.		Movement	Coefficient
13.		Transitions from collected walk to piaffe and from piaffe to passage	
14.	Between H & S S	Proceed in collected trot Track to the left	
15.	I R	Halt, rein back 4 steps, forward 4 steps, rein back 4 steps and immediately proceed in collected canter right Track to the right	
16.		Transitions from collected trot to halt and from the reinback to the collected canter right	
17.	BLK L	Change rein Pirouette to the right	
18.	K KAF	Flying change Collected canter	
19.	FLE L	Change rein Pirouette to the left	2
20.	E ESHC	Flying change Collected canter	
21.	CMRXVK	Extended walk	2
22.	K	Collected walk	
23.	A FXH	Collected canter On the diagonal 9 flying changes of leg every second stride	

No.		Movement	Coefficient
24.	MXK K	Change rein in extended canter Collected canter, flying change	
25.	A DG C	Down center line 3 counter changes half-pass to either side of the center line with change of leg at each change of direction; the first half-pass to the left and the last to the right of 4 strides; the 2 others of 8 strides Track to the right	
26.	MXK	On the diagonal 9 flying changes of leg every stride	
27.	A X	Down center line Halt, immobility, salute	

Collective Marks

No.	Movement	Coefficient
28.	Paces (freedom and regularity)	2
29.	Impulsion (desire to move forward, elasticity of the steps, suppleness of the back and engagement of the hindquarters)	2
30.	Submission (attention and confidence; harmony, lightness and ease of the movements; acceptance of the bridle and lightness of the forehand)	2
31.	Rider's position and seat; correctness and effect of the aids	2

Possible Points: 380

Arena for Dressage Competition 20 x 60m

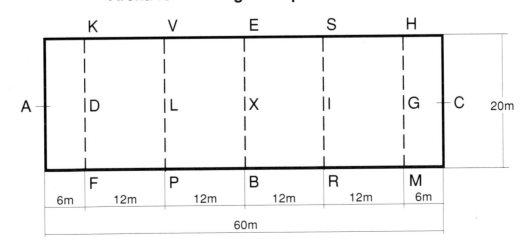

Left: Piaffe—the utmost collection while trotting in place.
A picture of great charisma; horse and rider have wonderful rapport. Despite intense concentration, a spark of joy leaps out and touches the spectators. Jean Bemelmans on the Hanoverian gelding Angelino by Archimedes at the 1987 German championships in Verden.

Above: Training the piaffe.
The Trakehner stallion Fabian by Donauwind, ridden by Dr. Reiner Klimke, has a natural aptitude for collection. The hindquarters are lowered and carry the weight. The stallion's neck is arched with good elevation, allowing the forearm to be angled almost horizontally.

Passage performed by a horse that made dressage history:
Otto Hofer (Switzerland), trainer of the Danish gelding Andiamo by May Sherif, the team silver medalist at the 1988 Olympics in Seoul, pictured here at the 1989 European dressage championships in Mondorf (Luxemburg) in a passage infused with the energy and forward drive of this powerful athlete.

Sven Rothenberger on Andiamo, winner of the 1990 dressage world cup in s'Hertogenbosch (Holland), in equally good passage with an accentuated moment of suspension.

Herbert Krug on the Swedish gelding Muskadeur performing movement 15 of the Grand Prix test at the 1984 Olympics in Los Angeles, the passage on the line I-R-B-X. Lovely expression, perfect balance following the turn to the right, and good harmony between horse and rider.

Johann Hinnemann on the Dutch gelding Ideaal by Doruto in an expressive and highly collected passage. This horse and rider won the team gold and individual bronze at the 1986 world dressage championships in Cedar Valley (Canada).

Sven Rothenberger continued Johann Hinnemann's string of successes on Ideaal: here is their picture-perfect extended trot at the world dressage championship in 1990 in Stockholm (Sweden), where they won the team gold and placed sixth in individual competition.

Michael Klimke on the Westphalian gelding Entertainer by Ehrensold in perfect salute stance.

Grand Prix

Should the trainer succeed in achieving with the horse with the demands of the piaffe and passage within the framework of Intermédiaire II—on the outside track—and if the horse has successfully mastered the flying change at every stride, then the rider can look forward with great confidence to the completion of training, safe in the knowledge that the horse is capable of all the movements of the Grand Prix.

With this, we have reached the threshold on which dressage riding can become art. The horse performs at the peak of his ability and places full trust in the harmonious aids of the rider.

Arena for Dressage Competition 20 x 60m

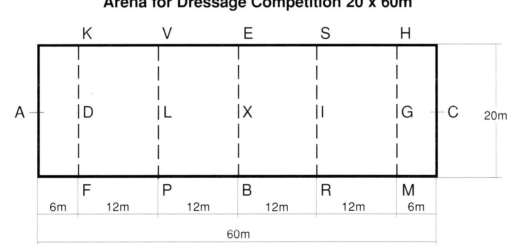

Grand Prix

Arena 20 x 60 m—Approximately 8 minutes.

			Coefficient
1.	A X	Enter in collected canter Halt, immobility, salute. Proceed in collected trot	
2.	C MXK KA	Track to the right Change rein in extended trot Collected trot	
3.	A FXH H	Collected canter Change rein in medium canter with flying change of leg at X Collected canter	
4.	C	Collected walk	
5.	M Between G & H	Turn right Half-pirouette to the right	
6.	Between G & M	 Half-pirouette to the left	
7.		The collected walk CMG(H)(M)G	
8.	GHS SP PFAKV	Collected trot Half-pass to the left Collected trot	
9.	VR RMCH	Half-pass to the right Collected trot	
10.	HXF	Change rein in extended trot	
11.	FAK	Passage	
12.	KVXRM	Change rein in extended walk	2
13.	MCH	Collected walk	
14.	H	Proceed in passage, transition from collected walk to passage	
15.	HSI	Passage	
16.	I	Piaffe 12 to 15 steps	
17.	I	Proceed in passage, transitions from passage to piaffe and from piaffe to passage	
18.	IRBX	Passage	
19.	X	Piaffe 12 to 15 steps	
20.	X	Proceed in passage, transitions from passage to piaffe and from piaffe to passage	
21.	XEV	Passage	
22.	V VKA	Proceed in collected canter Collected canter	
23.	AG	Down center line—5 counter changes of hand in half-pass to either side of the center line with flying change of leg at each change of direction; the first half-pass to the left and the last to the right of 3 strides; the 4 others of 6 strides finishing on the right leg	

			Coefficient
24.	C MXK K	Track to the right Change rein in extended canter Collected canter and flying change of leg	
25.	A L X	Down center line Pirouette to the left Flying change of leg	2
26.	I G C	Pirouette to the right Flying change of leg Track to the left	2
27.	HXF	On the diagonal 9 flying changes of leg every second stride (finishing on the right leg)	
28.	KXM	On the diagonal 15 changes of leg every stride (finishing on the left leg)	
29.	HXF F	Change rein in extended canter Collected canter and flying change of leg	
30.	A L	On center line Halt, rein back 6 steps, proceed in passage	
31.		Transition from collected canter to halt and from rein back to passage	
32.	LX	Passage	
33.	X	Piaffe 12 to 15 steps	
34.		Transitions from passage to piaffe and from piaffe to passage	
35.	XG	Passage	
36.	G	Halt, immobility, salute	

Collective Marks

37.	Paces (freedom and regularity)	2
38.	Impulsion (desire to move forward, elasticity of the steps, suppleness of the back and engagement of the hindquarters)	2
39.	Submission (attention and confidence; harmony, lightness and ease of the movements; acceptance of the bridle and lightness of the forehand)	2
40.	Rider's position and seat; correctness and effect of the aids	2

Possible Points: 470

This half-pass to the right across the full width of the arena demonstrates the peak of Grand Prix perfection. Almost nothing is more beautiful than the picture of a dancing horse! All the criteria for the half-pass are fulfilled nearly impeccably. The horse and rider have crossed the threshold to art. Nicole Uphoff on the Westphalian gelding Rembrandt by Romadur.

A nearly flawless piaffe.
Kyra Kyrklund (Finland) on the Danish stallion Matador by May Sherif in the 1988 Olympic Grand Prix in Seoul.

Right: Following a serious illness, Matador, with Kyra Kyrklund (Finland) riding, returned to international competition looking radiant. The Grand Prix Special at the 1990 world championships in Stockholm (Sweden): collected trot down the center line just before the transition to the final passage (movement 26 of the test). The pair won the silver medal in individual competition at the world championships in Stockholm and were winners at the 1991 dressage world cup in Paris.

At the 1988 Olympic Games in Seoul.

Top left: Robert Dover (USA) on the Hanoverian gelding Federleicht by Federgeist xx. An expressive final passage in the turn to the right in the 1988 Grand Prix test, with good flexion and bend.

Bottom left: The extended trot down the long side of the arena (movement 4 of the Grand Prix Special); good schwung and raising of the forehand. Robert Dover (USA) on Federleicht.

Above: Ann Kathrin Koth-Linsenhoff on the Swedish gelding Courage by Ceylon was a member of the victorious German team at the 1988 Seoul Olympics, and at the European championships in 1987 in Goodwood (England), and 1989 in Mondorf (Luxemburg). The rider and horse are in harmony at the extended trot.

An impressive passage down the center line, with energetic drive from the hindquarters, a good moment of suspension, and proper raising of the forehand. The rider's hands are in a nice low position.

Cynthia Ishoy (Canada) on the Hanoverian gelding Dynasty by Darling, the best Canadian pair at the 1986 world championships in Cedar Valley.

A piaffe that meets the requirements of the Classical high school of dressage: the horse lifts alternate diagonal pairs of feet with well-defined cadence. The rider keeps his hands low, facilitating the horse's proud neck carriage with the poll as the highest point.
Michael Klimke on the Westphalian gelding Entertainer by Ehrensold in 1989 in Wiesbaden.

Left: A canter pirouette as one seldom sees it, a flawless example of the Classical art of riding from our day.
Monica Theodorescu on the Westphalian gelding Ganimedes by Grnnhorn in 1990 in Balve.

Above: Monica Theodorescu on the Westphalian gelding Ganimedes by Grünhorn at the 1988 German championships in Verden. Few horses are capable of such expression in the extended trot.

Grand Prix Special

Arena 20 x 60m—Approximately 7 minutes

			Coefficient
1.	A X	Enter in collected canter Halt, immobility, salute. Proceed in collected trot	
2.	C HXF F	Track to the left Change rein in extended trot Collected trot	
3.	VXR RMC	Half-pass Collected trot	
4.	CHS SK KAF	Passage Extended trot Passage	
5.	FP PXS SHC	Collected trot Half-pass Collected trot	
6.	CMR RF FAK	Passage Extended trot Passage	
7.		Transitions from passage to extended trot and from extended trot to passage (tests 4 and 6)	
8.	KLBIH H	Extended walk Collected walk	2
9.	HCMG	Collected walk	
10.	G	Piaffe 12 to 15 steps	
11.	G	Proceed in passage. Transitions from collected walk to piaffe and from piaffe to passage	
12.	GHSI	Passage	
13.	I	Piaffe 12 to 15 steps	
14.	I	Proceed in passage. Transitions from passage to piaffe and from piaffe to passage	
15.	IRBX	Passage	
16.	XEVKAF	Collected canter left	
17.	FLE E	Half-pass in canter Flying change of leg	
18.	EIM M MCH	Half pass in canter Flying change of leg Collected canter	
19.	HXF	On the diagonal 9 changes of leg every second stride (finishing on left leg)	
20.	KXM	On the diagonal 15 changes of leg every stride (finishing on left leg)	
21.	HXF F	Change rein in extended canter Collected canter and flying change of leg	
22.	A D	Down center line Pirouette right	2
23.	Between D & G	On the center line 9 flying changes of leg every stride	
24.	G C	Pirouette left Track to the left	2
25.	HK K	Medium trot Collected trot	
26.	A L	Down center line Passage	
27.	I	Piaffe 12 to 15 steps	
28.		Transitions from collected trot to passage, from passage to piaffe	
29.	IG	Passage	
30.	G	Halt, immobility salute	

Collective Marks

		Coefficient
31.	Paces (freedom and regularity)	2
32.	Impulsion (desire to move forward, elasticity of the steps, suppleness of the back and engagement of the hindquarters)	2
33.	Submission (attention and confidence; harmony, lightness and ease of the movements; acceptance of the bridle and lightness of the forehand)	2
34.	Rider's position and seat; correctness and effect of the aids	2

Possible Points: 410

Arena for Dressage Competition 20 x 60m

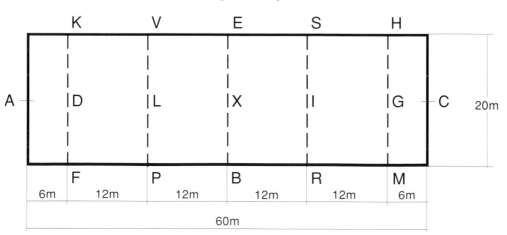

Dr. Reiner Klimke on the Hanoverian gelding Dux by Duellant at the 1968 Olympics in Mexico, where they won team gold and individual bronze medals. An extended canter with excellent action.

The Holsteiner gelding Corlandus by Cor de la Bryere is one of the equine personalities that have influenced international dressage competition. His rider, Margit Otto-Crepin, has accepted her horse's personality and adjusted to it with great sensitivity. The successes speak for themselves: after winning the 1987 European championship in Goodwood (England), she was runner-up at the 1989 championship in Mondorf (Luxemburg). Here, the final passage down the center line.

Margit Otto-Crepin and Corlandus narrowly missed winning the bronze medal at the 1990 world championship in Stockholm. With good elevation of the forehand and ears up, Corlandus displays all of his charm.

Nina Menkova (Russia) on the Russian stallion Dixon by Nabeg in piaffe in 1988 in Seoul. The confident and expressive piaffe and passage work of the Russian dressage riders' mounts is impressive.

Nina Menkova (Russia) on Dixon and Kyra Kyrklund on Matador gave each other an exciting run for the title at the 1991 dressage world cup in Paris. Second place was well earned.

The Hanoverian stallion Golfstrom by Grenadier, with Ann Kathrin Kroth-Linsenhoff riding, embodies a rare loyalty and willingness. The extended trot on the diagonal in 1990 in Balve: perfectly straight, with ears up and hindquarters strongly engaged.

Ann Kathrin Kroth-Linsenhoff on Golfstrom at the 1990 world championship in Stockholm: a confident passage with good neck carriage.

Nicole Uphoff on the Westphalian gelding Rembrandt by Romadur in the final piaffe on the center line (movement 27 of the Grand Prix Special), just seconds before their 1988 Olympic victory in Seoul.

Anne-Grethe Jensen on her Danish gelding Marzog by Herzog impressed the international dressage world with a fifth-place finish at the 1982 world championships in Lausanne (Switzerland). Marzog was only 9 at the time. The pair is pictured in the Grand Prix Special: the transition to the half-pass to the left. Very good flexion and bend.

After winning the 1983 European championship in Aachen, Anne-Grethe Jensen and Marzog won the individual silver medal at the 1984 Olympics in Los Angeles (USA). A picture of elegance and grace.

Top right: Dr. Uwe Shulten-Baumer on the Hanoverian gelding Madras by Monaco, individual and team European champion in 1981 in Laxenburg (Austria), in an expressive passage at the 1982 world championships in Lausanne (Switzerland), where they won the individual bronze medal.

Bottom right: Olympic Grand Prix Special in 1988 in Seoul.
Korean rider Jung-Kyun Suh, on the Danish gelding Pascal by The Stranger, exhibited great sensitivity. Pascal rewarded his rider with a harmonious performance that garnered 10th place.

Top left: Gabriela Grillo on the Trakehner gelding Ultimo by Heros, team champion and fourth in individual competition at the 1976 Olympics in Bromont: the passage in the turn to the left, approaching the long side of the arena. Good collection with distinct bend to the left. Especially noteworthy are the rider's low hand position and good closure of the right leg.

Bottom left: An expressive passage with a good moment of suspension: Gabriela Grillo on the Trakehner gelding Ultimo by Heros in the warm-up arena at the 1977 European championships in St. Gall (Switzerland), where the pair again won team gold and placed fourth in individual competition.

Above: Christine Stückelberger (Switzerland) on the Holsteiner gelding Granat by Consul at the 1976 Olympics in Bromont (Canada): nice elevation in the passage down the center line. This pair was an outstanding phenomenon in international dressage competition, winning the European championships in 1975 (Kiev) and 1977 (St. Gall), the Olympics in 1976 (Bromont), and the world championship in 1978 (Goodwood).

A happy rider and a contented horse leave the arena looking relaxed: Christine Stückelberger (Switzerland) on the Swedish stallion Gauguin de Lully by Chagall, individual bronze medalists at the 1988 Olympics in Seoul.

The Westphalian gelding Ahlerich by Angelo xx
followed in Granat's footsteps and replaced him
as world champion in 1982 in Lausanne
(Switzerland). The following photos show stages
of his development, from the first Grand Prix starts
to Olympic champion.

Ahlerich in training, in a snaffle bit: a radiant
equine personality. Absolutely effortless passage.

Top left: Ahlerich as a nine-year-old in 1980 in Rotterdam (Holland), in passage before a big audience; the winner in the Grand Prix Special.

Bottom left: A perfect piaffe in which everything is correct: lowered hindquarters, diagonal leg pairs lifted with distinct cadence, and the horse in proud carriage. Ahlerich in 1984 in Aachen.

Above: Ahlerich at the extended canter in 1984 in Los Angeles: a long canter stride with the right hind leg reaching well underneath, in the carriage of a Grand Prix horse.

Pages 92-93:
Ahlerich's 1984 Olympic victory in Los Angeles: a perfect example of schwung at the trot, from the collected to the extended trot.

World champion Ahlerich in 1985 in Copenhagen: the salute at the end of the Grand Prix Special.

The German championships in 1988 in Verden: a satisfied-looking Ahlerich leaves the arena. At age 17 he won his 7th German championship.

Louise Nathhorst (Sweden) on the Swedish gelding Dante in 1991 in Aachen; a remarkable degree of collection in piaffe.

Isabell Werth won the 1991 German dressage championship in Münster with the Hanoverian gelding Gigolo by Graditz, then only 8 years old.

Programs That Made History

The German Dressage Quadrille at the Olympic Games in Munich, 1972

One of the most magnificent presentations and one that lives on in memory, was the German quadrille at the Olympic Games in Munich in 1972. It was ridden by 12 of Germany's finest dressage riders in the celebration of the horse that marked the introduction of the closing ceremony of the XX. Olympiad Munich '72.

The best vaulting groups from the German national championships led the way, followed by Ernst Bachinger, instructor at the Spanish Riding School, who lead the Lippizan stallion Siglavy Modena through all the high school movements on the long rein. The sport of driving was represented by the eight best four-in-hand teams from the 1972 world championships, in front of 80,000 enthusiastic spectators in the Olympic stadium.

The highlight was the German dressage quadrille. A quadrille of such star quality had not been seen since World War II. Modelled after the German school quadrille of the Hannover Cavalry School, it embodied the classical equitation of our time. General Albert Stecken, then coach of the national dressage team, developed the program together with Willi Schultheis, incorporating into it the essential elements of the German school quadrille. George Theodorescu took over production and also assumed responsibility for the choice of music. As the 12 horses moved into final position, approaching the officials' stand in the Olympic stadium at the passage, the crowd applauded as though a world record had just been set. The horses had won their hearts.

The riders were, in the following order:

Dr. Reiner Klimke on York
Liselott Linsenhoff on Piaff
Wolfgang Haug on Lorlot
Karin Schlüter on Liostro
Josef Neckermann on Venetia
Ilsebill Becher on Mitsouko
Willi Schultheis on Armagnac
Inge Theodorescu on Marzio
Walter Günther on Partisan
Gabriela Grillo on Honduras
Harry Boldt on Ariadne
Eva-Maria Pracht on Mazepa

In later years, the Olympic dressage quadrille, sometimes with different but equally skilled riders, exhibited several more times, including in 1973 in Aachen and Amsterdam, in 1974 in Dortmund and Berlin, in 1985 again in Berlin, and in 1986 in Kronberg. The group was dissolved after that, and the form of the German dressage quadrille will live on with new music and the most successful German dressage riders of today's generation.

The Pas de Deux

The two best dressage horses in the world from 1982 to 1986 performed a pas de deux in 1985 in Stuttgart's Schleyer Hall that in its symmetry of movement and harmony of presentation elicited thunderous applause from the audience. This pas de deux was presented again in Gothenborg in 1986.

Anne-Grethe Jensen on the Danish gelding Marzog by Herzog and Dr. Reiner Klimke on the Westphalian gelding Ahlerich by Angelo xx. A flawless execution of shoulder-in down the center line.

A pas de deux at the finals of the 1986 jumper world cup in Gothenburg (Sweden): a perfect extended trot. Anne-Grethe Jensen on Marzog and Dr. Reiner Klimke on Ahlerich.

The Pas de Trois

The pas de trois in 1988 in Martin Schleyer Hall in Stuttgart was a presentation that made history. To mark Ahlerich's retirement from competition following the Olympic Games in Seoul in 1988, Seoul silver medalist Margit Otto-Crepin (France) on the Holsteiner gelding Corlandus, bronze medal-winner Christine Stückelberger (Switzerland) on the Swedish stallion Gauguin de Lully, and Dr. Reiner Klimke on the Westphalian gelding Ahlerich demonstrated the beauty and harmony of dressage in a pas de trois.

A flawless extended trot, as though the horses had worked it out amongst themselves beforehand: the ultimate expression of movement in three quite different horses, with an almost perfectly synchronized step. From left to right: Corlandus, Ahlerich, and Gauguin de Lully.

Canter on the right lead down the center line. From left to right: Corlandus, Ahlerich, and Gauguin de Lully in the pas de trois.

The Old Masters

Above: Henry Chammartin (Switzerland) on the Swedish gelding Wolfdietrich by Darladier at the 1968 Olympics in Mexico.
Between 1955 and 1965, Henry Chammartin was the most successful championship rider in dressage. He won his biggest victories with the three Swedish horses Wöhler, Woermann, and Wolfdietrich. On Wöhler he won the FEI championships in 1955 in Thun (Switzerland), 1958 in Wiesbaden, and 1959 in St. Gall (Switzerland). He won the European dressage championships with Wolfdietrich in 1963 and 1965 in Copenhagen (Denmark), and the 1964 Tokyo (Japan) Olympics on Woermann.

Top right: Riding the Westphalian gelding Mariano by Ramzes, Josef Neckermann won individual silver and team gold medals at the 1968 Olympics in Mexico. Two years prior, at the first dressage world championships in Bern (Switzerland), he experienced what must have been the greatest triumph of his sports career: the gold in both team and individual competition.

Bottom right: Josef Neckermann on the Holsteiner mare Venetia by Anblick xx at the 1972 Olympics in Munich: the bronze medal in individual competition and silver with the German team.

Above: Marianne Gossweiler (Switzerland) on the Holsteiner gelding Stephan, in a textbook piaffe. With members of the Swiss team, the pair won Olympic silver medals in 1964 in Tokyo and 1968 in Mexico.

Top right: On the Swedish stallion Piaff by Gaspari, Liselott Linsenhoff was the most successful woman dressage rider from 1969 to 1972. She was the European champion and team gold medalist in both 1969 and 1971 in Wolfsburg. In 1972, riding Piaff, Liselott Linsenhoff became the first woman to win the individual dressage competition at the Olympic Games.

Bottom right: Piaff did justice to his name. His piaffe was considered the best of his day.

Above: Elena Petuschkova (USSR) on the Russian stallion Pepel by Piligrim won the team gold and individual silver in 1972 in Munich. The pair celebrated their biggest win in 1970 in Aachen. There they were world champions in individual competition and also won the team gold.

Top right: Dr. Reiner Klimke on the Hanoverian gelding Mehmed by Ferdinand at the 1976 Olympics in Bromont (Canada). In his heyday, Mehmet was regarded as the horse with the best basic gaits. He was European champion in 1973 in Aachen and world champion in 1974 in Copenhagen (Denmark). As part of the German team he won the team gold at the 1969, 1971, and 1973 European championships, at the 1974 world championship, and at the 1976 Olympics.

Bottom right: Dr. Uwe Schulten-Baumer on the Hanoverian gelding Slibovitz by Servus, runner-up at the 1978 world championships in Goodwood (England). Their expression and consistency made them an outstanding pair.

Above: Harry Boldt on the Hanoverian gelding Woyzek by Wunsch II in the pirouette to the right at the 1976 Olympics in Bromont (Canada). From 1975 to 1979 this pair was the reliable mainstay of the German dressage team, winning team gold medals at the 1976 European championship in Kiev (USSR), the 1976 Olympics in Bromont (Canada), the 1977 European championship in St. Gall (Switzerland), the 1978 world championship at Goodwood (England), and the 1979 European championship in Aarhus (Denmark). In addition, Harry Boldt and Woyzek won silver medals in individual competition in 1975 in Kiev, 1976 in Bromont, 1977 in St. Gall, and 1979 in Aarhus.

Top right: Uwe Sauer, on the Holsteiner stallion Montevideo by Marlon xx, was a member of the victorious German team at the European championships in 1983 in Aachen and 1985 in Copenhagen (Denmark), and at the 1984 Olympics in Los Angeles (USA).

Bottom right: Anne-Grethe Jensen on Danish gelding Marzog by Herzog in a masterful pirouette to the left at the 1986 world championships in Cedar Valley (Canada). Good absorption of weight in the hindquarters. The horse moves around the hindquarters in as small a circle as possible, with a clear three-beat rhythm and distinct flexion and bend. With their elegance and lightness, this pair gave the dressage world of the 1980's new impetus: European champion in 1983 in Aachen, world champion in 1986 in Cedar Valley, silver medalist at the 1984 Olympics in Los Angeles, and winner of the first dressage world cup in 1986 in s'Hertogenbosch (Holland).

Champions of Dressage

Olympic Medalists from 1912 to 1988

1912 Stockholm/S
1. C. Graf Bond — S
2. G. A. Boltensten — S
3. H. v. Blixen-Finecke — S

No team competition

1920 Antwerp/B
1. J. Lundblad — S
2. K. B. Sandström — S
3. Graf v. Rosen — S

No team competition

1924 Paris/F
1. E. de Linder — S
2. K. B. Sandström — S
3. Francois Lesage — F

No team competition

1928 Amsterdam/NL
1. C. F. Frhr. v. Langden — D
2. Marion — F
3. Ragnar Olson — S

Team
1. D
2. S
3. NL

1932 Los Angeles/USA
1. François Lesage — F
2. Marion — F
3. Hiram Tuttle — USA

Team
1. F
2. S
3. USA

1936 Berlin/D
1. Heinz Pollay — D
2. Friedrich Gerhard — D
3. Alois Podhajsky — A

Team
1. D
2. F
3. S

1948 London/GB
1. Hans Moser — CH
2. A. R. Jousseaume — F
3. Gustav A. Boltenstern — S

Team
1. F
2. USA
3. P

1952 Helsinki/N
1. Henri St. Cyr — S
2. Liz Hartel — DK
3. A. R. Jousseaume — F

Team
1. S
2. CH
3. BRD

1956 Stockholm/S
1. Henri St. Cyr — S
2. Liz Hartel — DK
3. Liselott Linsenhoff — BRD

Team
1. S
2. BRD
3. CH

1960 Rome/I
1. Sergey Filatow — USSR
2. Gustav Fischer — CH
3. Josef Neckermann — BRD

No team competition

1964 Tokyo
1. Henri Chammartin — CH
2. Harry Boldt — BRD
3. Sergey Filatow — USSR

Team
1. BRD
2. CH
3. USSR

1968 Mexico
1. Ivan Kizimov — USSR
2. Josef Neckermann — BRD
3. LDr. Reiner Klimke — BRD

Team
1. BRD
2. USSR
3. CH

1972 Münich/BRD
1. Liselott Linsenhoff — BRD
2. Elena Petushkova — USSR
3. Josef Neckermann — BRD

Team
1. USSR
2. BRD
3. S

1976 Montreal/CAN
1. Christine Stückelberger — CH
2. Harry Boldt — BRD
3. Dr. Reiner Klimke — BRD

Team
1. BRD
2. CH
3. USA

1980 Moscow/USSR
1. Elisabeth Theurer — A
2. Yuri Kowschow — USSR
3. Viktor Ugrimow — USSR

Team
1. USSR
2. Bulgaria
3. Rumania

1984 Los Angeles/USA
1. Dr. Reiner Klimke — BRD
2. Anne Grethe Jensen — DK
3. Otto Hofer — CH

Team
1. BRD
2. CH
3. S

1988 Seoul
1. Nicole Uphoff — BRD
2. Margit Otto-Crepin — FRA
3. Christine Stückelberger — CH

Team
1. BRD
2. CH
3. CAN

World Champions since 1966

1966 Bern/CH
1. Dr. Josef Neckermann — BRD
2. Harry Boldt — BRD
3. Dr. Reiner Klimke — BRD

Team
1. BRD
2. CH
3. USSR

1970 Aachen/BRD
1. Elena Petushkova — USSR
2. Liselott Linsenhoff — BRD
3. Ivan Kizimov — USSR

Team
1. USSR
2. BRD
3. DDR

1974 Kopenhagen/DK
1. Dr. Reiner Klimke — BRD
2. Liselott Linsenhoff — BRD
3. Elena Brumel-Petushkova — USSR

Team
1. BRD
2. USSR
3. CH

1978 Goodwood/GB
1. Christine Stückelberger — CH
2. Uwe Schulten-Baumer — BRD
3. Jennie Loriston Clarke — GB

Team
1. BRD
2. CH
3. USSR

1982 Lausanne/CH
1. Dr. Reiner Klimke — BRD
2. Christine Stückelberger — CG
3. Uwe Schulten-Baumer — BRD

Team
1. BRD
2. CH
3. DK

1986 Cedar Valley/CAN
1. Anne Grete Jensen — DK
2. Christine Stückelberger — CH
3. Johann Hinnemann — BRD

Team
1. BRD
2. NL
3. CH

1990 Stockhold/S
1. Nicole Uphoff — BRD
2. Kyra Kyrklund — SF
3. Monica Theodorescu — BRD

Team
1. BRD
2. USSR
3. CH

European Champions from 1963 to 1989

1963 Copenhagen/DK
1. Henri Chammartin — CH
2. Harry Boldt — BRD
3. Henri Chammartin — CH

Team
1. GB
2. RUM

1965 Copenhagen/DK
1. Henri Chammartin — CH
2. Harry Boldt — BRD
3. Reiner Klimke — BRD

Team
1. BRD
2. CH
3. USSR

1967 Aachen/BRD
1. Reiner Klimke — BRD
2. Ivan Kizimov — USSR
3. Harry Boldt — BRD

Team
1. BRD
2. USSR
3. CH

1969 Wolfsburg/BRD
1. Liselott Linsenhoff — BRD
2. Ivan Kizimov — USSR
3. Josef Nechermann — BRD

Team
1. BRD
2. DDR
3. USSR

1971 Wolfsburg/BRD
1. Liselott Linsenhoff — BRD
2. Josef Neckermann — BRD
3. Ivan Kizimov — USSR

Team
1. BRD
2. USSR
3. S

1973 Aachen/BRD
1. Reiner Klimke — BRD
2. Elena Petushkova — USSR
3. Ivan Kalita — USSR

Team
1. BRD
2. USSR
3. CH

1975 Kiev/USSR
1. Christine Stückelberger — CH
2. Harry Boldt — BRD
3. Karin Schlüter — BRD

Team
1. BRD
2. U — SSR
3. CH

1977 St. Gallen/CH
1. Christine Stückelberger — CH
2. Harry Boldt — BRD
3. Uwe Schulten-Baumer — BRD

Team
1. BRD
2. CH
3. USSR

1979 Aarhus/DK
1. Elisabeth Theurer — A
2. Christine Stückelberger — CH
3. Harry Boldt — BRD

Team
1. BRD
2. USSR
3. CG

1981 Luxemburg/A
1. Uwe Schulten-Baumer — BRD
2. Christine Stückelberger — CH
3. Gabriela Grillo — BRD

Team
1. BRD
2. CH
3. USSR

1983 Aachen/BRD
1. Anne-Grethe Jensen — DK
2. Reiner Klimke — BRD
2. Uwe Sauer — BRD

Team
1. BRD
2. DK
3. CH

1985 Copenhagen/DK
1. Reiner Klimke — BRD
2. Otto Hofer — CH
3. Anne-Grether Jensen — DK

Team
1. BRD
2. DK
3. USSR

1987 Goodwood/GB
1. Margit Otto-Crepin — FRA
2. Ann Kathrin Linsenhoff — BRD
3. Johan Hinnemann — BRD

Team
1. BRD
2. CH
3. NL

1989 Mondorf/L
1. Nicole Uphoff — BRD
2. Margit Otto-Crepin — FRA
3. Ann Kathrin Linsenhoff — BRD